ALL RIGHTS RESERVED. NO PART OF THIS BOOK MAY BE REPRODUCED IN ANY FORM OR BY ANY ELECTRONIC OR MECHANICAL MEANS INCLUDING INFORMATION STORAGE AND RETRIEVAL SYSTEMS - EXCEPT IN THE CASE OF BRIEF QUOTATIONS EMBODIED IN CRITICAL ARTICLES OR REVIEWS - WITHOUT PERMISSION IN WRITING FROM ITS PUBLISHER MIKAELA WOODS

"The beauty of aquatic life is a reminder of the delicate balance of nature and our responsibility to protect it."

Once upon a time in the deep blue sea

Lived many creatures, so wondrous and free

Narwhals with their long, pointy tooth

Belugas with their white skin, so smooth

Jellyfish, so pretty, they glimmer and glow

Coral, so colourful, in the current they flow

Seahorses, they prance and they sway

HUMPBACK WHALES, THEY SING
A SONG NIGHT AND DAY

Hammerhead sharks with their heads so wide

Octopus, they change colour and hide

Manta rays, they glide through the water

Starfish, with their arms, they never falter

Manatees, they munch on the plants

Orcas, they swim in big family chants

And last but not least, the eels in the reef, They slither and slide, without any grief

These creatures of the sea are all unique

And together they make a world that's full of mystique.

Manufactured by Amazon.ca
Bolton, ON